POEMS   LETTERS

Second Chance

RANDOM THOUGHTS

Karl T. Woods

AuthorHouse™
1663 Liberty Drive
Bloomington, IN 47403
www.authorhouse.com
Phone: 833-262-8899

Because of the dynamic nature of the Internet, any web addresses or links contained in this book may have changed
since publication and may no longer be valid. The views expressed in this work are solely those of the author and do not
necessarily reflect the views of the publisher, and the publisher hereby disclaims any responsibility for them.

Any people depicted in stock imagery provided by Getty Images are models,
and such images are being used for illustrative purposes only.
Certain stock imagery © Getty Images.

This book is printed on acid-free paper.

ISBN: 978-1-6655-4549-5 (sc)
978-1-6655-4548-8 (e)

Library of Congress Control Number: 2021923945

Print information available on the last page.

Published by AuthorHouse 11/26/2021

authorHOUSE®

Dedicated to God my loving Creator
His Son Jesus Christ
And the Holy Spirit
Whom guides me through
My earthly journey

TABLE OF CONTENTS

Preface

This is my third book of poetry. I wasn't sure if I would get a third book written at all. I have been battling Multiple Myeloma an incurable blood cancer for the past four years. Some days my brain won't connect the dots. Writing anything that makes sense is often a challenge.

Writing Second Chance has been a labor of love to say the least and has been very therapeutic for me as I battle the effects of chemo therapy. My chemo brain or brain fog as it is called often makes every task a challenge. Getting Second Chance written and published is what I needed to do to fight the cancer and to challenge myself.

Many of the of the poems in the Second Chance were developed from putting together random thoughts I had written down over the years. Others were unfinished poems that lived on paper for years. It was those random thoughts or bits and pieces I call them that came into play. It took months but somehow I was able to use them to put a complete poem together. Every thought counted.

So, I pushed through it all and made it happen the best I could. One foot in front of the other, one day after another. I could have easily just chill out and done nothing all day so when I say push, I do mean push myself.

Any cancer patient will tell you the same thing. If we don't push ourselves and keep our PMA (positive mental attitude) together nothing will happen and we will waste away.
Writing has become more therapeutic for me than ever before, who knew, I guess cancer.

Anything I can do to push myself that challenges my brain I do. Thus the watercolors which I hope you enjoy. They came about from being cooped up at home avoiding Covid out in the wild.

I aways need to challenge my brain to connect the dots before the chemo and/or cancer renders it useless. Please pray tor me…I thank you in advance.

I thought I would do something totally different with Second Chance.
As I was working on putting the poems in an order that seemed to flow I discovered why not break them up into sections. First, the romantic, then the deeper more introspective poems, and finally the letters and a bit of satire.

And for color, add a few paintings throughout with the bulk at the end. All things considered I felt my brain could manage that process rather than mixing the poems and paintings up.

The most important thing is that you the reader enjoy them. So, sit back with your beverage and dig in.

About the Author

Karl is a native Californian who grew up in Los Angeles. He currently lives in San Diego, CA. where he continued to write and currently trying his hand with watercolors as well. The pandemic has brought about many changes for us all.

Karl has achieved numerous awards through poetry contest he has entered over the years and has been published in three Anthologies.

His first two books Secret's of my Heart and In a Better Place Now were well received. Second Chance, the third in the trilogy seamlessly blends into the authors passion for exploring the beauty of life.

LOOKING FORWARD

SECOND CHANCE

The Bible says they who wait on the Lord
Shall mount up with wings like eagles
Be patient, and wait upon the Lord
He searches our heart and tries our reins
He knows what we need before we ask
He answers prayers in His time not ours
Truly, there is test, test, then treasure
I always keep my faith in Him
He is able to do abundantly above
All that I could ask or think
He has given me a second chance at life
He found it in his grace and mercy
To give my cancer remission for now
He gave me back the gift of music
He let's me sing with joy
And write with passion
He brought back quality of life
He has given this humble servant
A second chance
And I am so grateful

LIVE WISE

People are tough
But life is fragile
Don't know one minute to the next
Count your blessings
Moment by moment
While the blood
Is running warm in your veins
Be thankful for all things
Small or large
Today is the right day
Tomorrow is promised to no one
Life is fragile
Treat it with respect
Love as much as you can
Give from your heart

TRUST

Our love for each other
Is what holds us together
It is a dream come true
We share our thoughts and feelings
Without doubt
We trust each other
Without question
We support and encourage each other
As if we are being reborn each day
You are my one true love
And I pray that I mean as much to you
As you mean to me

WELCOMING

Trust in me
As I will trust in you
There are few people in my life
That inspire me as much as you
There are things in life we all hope for
For me, it's your love
You are what I think of most
Like a welcoming
Your passion reaches
Deep within my heart

COME BACK

The days are long
Without you in my life
Time seems to stand still
Before my very eyes
Without you
I am incomplete
May a candle of love
Stay lit in our hearts
To guide our love
To a deeper truth

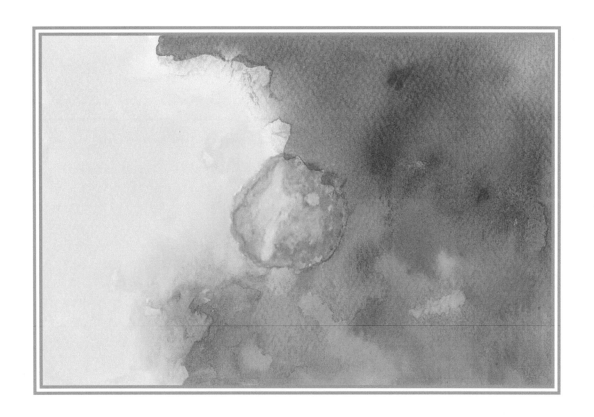

SUNBURST

DAYBREAK

As I sat on my patio this morning
Watching a beautiful sunrise
Usher in a new day
I'm thinking about us
The sunrise not only speaks of a new day
But brings to mind new hopes
New dreams and desires
Of a good day, and a brighter tomorrow
I am thankful for you today
And dream of a bright tomorrow for us
A tomorrow where we allow
Our trust and admiration for each other
To grow and flourish into a beautiful friendship
Unencumbered by the weight of the world
By the weight of our fears
And the weight of others

NEW BEGINNING

You came into my life
When I needed you the most
You came when my spirit was weakening
When my faith in humanity, life, and love
Was coming into question
You brought so much joy into my life
At a time when I needed it the most
You enrich my life and lift my spirit
I enjoy seeing your warm and sincere smile
I enjoy hearing your voice speak kind words
I love the thoughtfulness you give
From your loving and tender heart
And the icing on the cake
Of course is your adorable personality
And that you are gorgeous
All combined, you are a treasure
And a blessing to all who know you
I am so glad you are in my life Amor
A treasure and blessing indeed

LITE HEARTED

You make me feel
Like dancing on a cloud
You make me feel
Like shouting out loud
You make me feel
I wanna sing my song
You make me feel
Our love will never go wrong
I told you to never look away
Yes I told you baby
That I'm here to stay
I told you girl
I'm gonna carry you away
Just wait and see darling
Yes, just wait for that day

THINKING OUT LOUD

I'm just like you
Looking for a meaningful relationship
With friendship at its core
And love as its cornerstone
So you can build a life
Beyond your wildest imagination
I see that dream in you
As I look into your eye's
And peruse your soul
How I long for youth again
Every time I see you
So I can be part of your dreams
And the man you long for
To help you build that wonderful life
We would be wise to remember
If friendship is its core
Let's grab on to it
And dream of what if

THE TIMING OF THE RAIN

It was well past midnight
As we sat by the fire light
I gazed into your eyes
And you held me tight
You promised me it would be alright
If I just held you right
As if tomorrow was not in sight
You're my baby and you mean so much
Soft and sweet is your tender touch
You know it hasn't been easy for me lately
Lots of dark and stormy days
But your love I'll never throw away
If we walk downtown on this rainy day
All the water couldn't wash this moment away
While we splash in puddles up and down the street
Laughing and joking skipping our feet
Holding hands and holding on tight
Can we watch raindrops fall into the night
Every second with you is sure to be right
I'll hold you in my arms darling
I'll hold hold you your way
Well into the light of day
As we move forward day by day
Your love makes me stronger
While it lights our way
I can never thank you enough darling
For your warm and tender touch
And I'll always tell you
I love you so much

LOVE ANEW

I always thought I knew love
But you showed me love anew
I always thought I knew love
But your love
Brought new meaning to my life
When I think of love
I think of you
When I think of the emptiness in my heart
I think of your love
Taking its place

MOONRISE

HOPEFUL

This year I am especially grateful and thankful
Because you are in my life
You have brought so much happiness into my life
I can hardly find the words to express my feelings
You are a sign of greater things to come
A sign of better days ahead
There is a richness and beauty
That flows from your heart to mine
You inspire me
Your presence keeps me lifted up and encouraged
I look forward
To all the wonderful moments
And experiences we will share
As we build our friendship together
And we will build it with loving hearts
As we feel the warmth from within

WAIT ON GOD

It will not always
Work out like you planned
But God planned it with what you need
Being patient to understand
Is the key and the lesson learned
Wait on God
Listen for His voice
Listen for His calling

STAY STRONG

In our darkest hours
And perilous times
There is a light
That shines in all of us
Often we don't realize it
Or even see it
For various reasons
It seems to boil down
To one thing
Fear
Fear of the unknown
Fear of the situation itself
Stay strong
Rise above all that you fear
At the end of the day
Most of what we fear
Never happens anyway
You know I'm right
Stay up
Stay strong
Pray much
And watch the magic happen

DO IT NOW

Everyone must tackle
Their issues of life
In a way
That comforts their soul
And eases their mind
The key is to do it quickly
Run the gauntlet
So you don't stay
In a state of despair too long
Your health, outlook, and spirit
Depends on it

QSO

When you need
A dose of sonic elixir
Look for
QSO
Quality Snake Oil
The band you can
Count on
Time after time
It's good for your soul

DISCIPLINE

A demon is something
I have to slay
Weakness is merely something
I have to overcome
Without discipline
I am half the man
I need to be

WHAT DOES?

It requires
Unwavering faith
And
The ultimate
Sacrifice

MY MOVE

It only hurts
When I screw up
No worries
I'm still in the game
I have a token
To play

MOVE ON

Get over it
And
Get on with it
Step up
Or
Step back

BE GRATEFUL

We don't get
What we think we deserve
We get what grace provides
God saved us
And provides for us
By His grace, mercy, and love
Now, don't you feel blessed?

MAGICAL GARDEN

LET US PRAY

May the spirit of God
Always move
In and through
Our relationship
To keep us
Strong and working
Together

AS ONE

Loving you comes easy
So natural from my heart to yours
Loving you comes easy
I can't pretend of something so real
Everyday when I think of you
I think of our hearts as one

SPIRIT OF THE SEASON

I give thanks everyday
For the blessings that fill my life
Especially for the small things
Because they are really huge in my mind
They help me appreciate
And prepare for the big things to come
The Thanksgiving and Christmas season
Are extra special for me
The time of the year
When I give more thanks
And feel more grateful than usual
The weather cools
And the warmth of the season
Seems to come from within
A time to share with family and friends
A time to reflect on all the goodness in my life
A time to embrace the special someone
With even greater passion
As the air fills with nutmeg and cinnamon

SENTIMENTAL

Call me sentimental
You would be right
I am, and very much so
I will never forget our first kiss
And I pray a prelude to many more
Under the glow of Christmas lights
After a wonderful day of fun
Your lips pressed against mine
Was a dream come true for me
How I have longed to hold you in my arms
Feel your heart beat against my chest
And taste your sweet tender lips
But I never want to rush or push you
I enjoy letting time takes its course
And it did
Our embrace happened naturally
Our kisses were filled with compassion
They were tender and warm
And spoke of the passion between us
Without uttering a word
Your touch was soft, sweet, and reassuring
And without saying a word
Spoke of how much you care for me
I am so grateful you are in my life
You take such good care of me, always
And I will always do the same for you
You share your heart and thoughts
With me in trust
Knowing I will return in kind
The joy you have brought into my life
Is immeasurable
You are an amazing woman
I just thought you should know

GROWING FOREST

JUST ANOTHER FARIY TALE

Once upon a time
There was a woman
Who was fed up
With the foolishness of the men in her life
Every time she got a boyfriend
Her life would become filled
With grief and drama
Then one day she realized
There is a man in her life
Sitting quietly in her midst
That adores her very much
He willingly fills her life
With understanding, admiration, and laugher
Without the grief and drama
Oh, what a joy she thought
She though, I'll call him
My imaginary boyfriend
Keep him close at heart
And life will be good
He will never leave nor forsake me
And she'll never feel alone
And she lived happily ever after

The End

VAIN WOMAN

Last act of a vain woman
What else can she do
Can't see her life
Before her own eye's
But she's telling me what to do
Last act of a desperate man
Trying hard not to give up on love
Fighting off his baby's demons
As every smart man should
Cause you know
There's two sides to every story
But you never considered mine
Just another vain woman
Thinking of herself all the time
Vanity has made you so blind
You're in your own world
Most all the time
Eye's wide open
But mind closed shut
Keep living that way
You gonna need a whole lot of luck
I can see the emptiness
In your soul
Your eye's paint the picture
Of a heart so cold
You thought we were doing well
And you looked so surprised
When I handed you my resignation letter
And said goodbye
Cause you know
There's two sides to every story
But you never considered mine
Just another vain woman
Thinking of herself
Most all the time

COME AND GO

Your wishes and whims
Much to my chagrin
You baffle me again
It's not what you do
Rather how you do it
How you come and how you go
That troubles me so

PAINTING THE GRASS GREEN #1

Looking at folks day by day
I see the front on their faces along the way
The faking it to make it
Pretending all is well
Faking a smile, it's easy to tell
Painting the grass green
Keeping up the front
Hoping that sink hole
Doesn't swallow them up
Putting on the airs
Trying not to show the pain
Keeping up the front
Playing the game
Taking a journey inward
Looking to the outward
Dressing up the outer wear
What about the inner wear
Inward man keeping up the front
Reaching for the brass ring
Like a carrot on a stick
Pretending to be happy faking a smile
Keeping up the front all the while
It's all in reach, you know it's true
Painting the grass green will not get get you through
Keeping up the front won't do

NEW GROWTH

PAINTING THE GRASS GREEN #2

What has my life become
Everyday I keep painting the grass green
Keeping up the front
I get pushed and pulled here and there
And nowhere I get pushed seems fair
Over and over, day after day
The grass doesn't get greener along the way
I see the front on their faces
The faking it to make it
Pretending all is well
Faking a smile, it's easy to tell
But surely living a private hell
Painting the grass green
Keeping up the front
Trying not to show the pain
All the while playing the game
Keeping up the front
Barely staying sane
It's all in reach, I know it's true
Keeping up the front will have to do
So busy doing for other's
I've lost my way
And wonder when will I reclaim my day
Believing the lies I know are not true
Spinning and going nowhere
While my life goes slowly blue
I gotta be blunt
Man, it's a crazy scene
Stop believing all those lies
And painting the grass green

THE LAST EDGE

You know how folks say
I gonna stop doing this or that?
Well maybe not today
But I'm gonna do it
You just wait and see
We wake up the next morning
Full of good intent
And that Jones still has us in its grip
And we think, I just need to take the edge off
And I'll be good to go
I'll start after that
Man, that thinking doesn't work
Later that day you're off the races again
And the cycle continues
Ya gotta grow a pair and stop doing it
You know, whatever it is you are doing
It's just a form of addiction, period
It doesn't matter what it is
A friend told me something real simple years ago
He had recently quit drinking alcohol
Hey bro, if you don't wanna drink
Just don't buy alcohol
I apply that philosophy to everything
Try it, it works
Along with a determined mind set

WHY

Why
Don't we love
With the passion
We once shared?
We must never forget
The passion
Which brought us together
I am always willing to try
But I can't do it alone
I will not give up on you
Please, don't give up on me
Our love for each other
Is still a dream come true

CIRCLES

In the minutes and the hours
When we first met
I told you things
I hoped you'd never forget
As the years passed by
Your heart seemed to forget
All the sweetness
I have not forgotten yet
Where did we go wrong
What page did we not turn
Where did we go wrong
Does your heart still yearn
It caught me by surprise
The way things turned
Can't you feel my love for you still burns
The love in my eyes should lead the way
But you put it off for another day
Life always seems to get in our way
We can't gain ground and make it stay
Going in circles is our only way
Where did we go wrong
What page have we not turned
Where did we go wrong
Does your heart still yearn

B MOVIE

Lately, my life has been full of ups and downs
Mostly downs though the ups do come around
Can't help thinking my life is like a B movie
Strange day's come and sit for a spell
When they gonna leave it's hard to tell
I sit and tell myself well, what the hell
I've got no story left to tell
Cause I left my life
In the pockets of yesterdays pants
With a tarnished copper penny
I left there by chance
Times have gotta change soon
They can't stay the same
Playing in this B movie is a tough game
The player's are all there
Though the faces change
And my tarnished copper penny
Still looks the same
Oh, it's not as bad as I make it out to be
It seems I've become my own worst enemy
It's time I open my eye's and see what is real
This is my reality and that's the deal

EMOTIONAL FAILURE

You push away the good
And embrace the bad
What on earth
Is going on in your mind
Then you wonder why I walk away
And question your sincerity
You wonder why
I don't take you seriously
I don't know what you have become
But it's not becoming of you

CHANGE MY MIND

I won't let you control my roll
I'm taking back the real estate in my head
You won't beat me down to the ground
You have lost yourself in living
And lost life along the way
It's hard to fight the wars in your head
While enduring the battles of your life
I've given you the moon
If you want the stars
You have to reach for them
Cause the songs of my heart
Aren't the ones you're singing
And the song in my head
Is not the one you're hearing

OVER THE WALL

PATCH WORK

Sometimes relationships
Get a little tricky
And we find ourselves trying
To fit between the spaces
Of each others life
Fit between the crack's
I'm just a piece of the puzzle
Another piece for you to figure out
Go on, say it
I'm gonna hear it one way or another
One day or another
Because you won't stop
Until you get it said
Right, wrong, or indifferent
But be aware
Don't speak of your moves much
People these days don't want to hear it
You just may get your feelings hurt
It really only matters to you

THE LAST VESTIGE #1

The older this hopeless romantic gets
It has become evident
That it gets
Increasing hopeless to be a romantic
The loves of my life
Continually remind me

THE LAST VESTIGE #2

The older this hopeless romantic gets
It's hard not to realize
That it gets increasingly harder
To be a romantic
My loves have continued
To let me down
It's a two way street
I look for the error of my ways
Especially, my part in the play
Does anyone meet half way anymore
Or do we all want our way
Anytime, every time, all the time
Love is a demanding emotion
Engaging yet frustrating
That requires patience and nurturing

ONCE AGAIN

I don't know what's on your mind
But every time I need you
You make me lose mine
Every time I need you
You have something better to do
You make it hard to trust you
Along the way
So I expect nothing better another day
You say you're sorry but that gets old
When I need someone to trust and hold
Guess I'll do what I need to do
Keep you in the dark and be blue
Then I will expect nothing from you
And there will be no more once again

RECKONING

Today is my day of reckoning
To realize it's not my plan
But God's plan
He knows whats best for me
He has opened the door
Cleared a path for me to grow
With renewed understanding
His grace
Put me right where I need to be
In the right place, at the right time
So He can save me
Today I must realize this
And remember to toe the line
All the time
This requires unwavering faith
And the ultimate sacrifice
This I must reckon
As poison is pumped into my body
To kill the cancer
That tries to kill me now
I only need vices when I'm to weak
To accept the challenge
Of change and growth
Pray for me

LIFE 101

When I get outta here
I'll bless you from above
I'll be your Angel
I hope you learn
My lessons for you
Before I go
As a dad, I hold my truths very dear
You don't always want to hear them
But they are real
Trust me sometimes
They are the truth
Learn your lessons in your youth
As you age they will come to pass
As I push up daisies from the grass
A father wants the best for his children
No matter what the cost
If they will only listen
And give pause
Don't be haste in your judgement
You are still young
And have not quite adjusted
You'll understand what truth is true
And you'll teach the same to your children
Unbeknownst to you

NJAMBI

There is so much I could write about you
But yet I had not written a word
By the time my second book was published
With no mention of you
Your reaction shook me to my core
And I had to ask myself why
I had not written a poem for my little sister
Sometimes seeing you as my rock
Has clouded my judgement
Though you are strong and wise
You are still flesh and blood
With weakness as well as strengths
You feel pain and joy as we all do
But this is no excuse on my part
I could write a book about you
I could write a book of all your successes over hardship
And how you always make me laugh and smile
I could tell the story of our childhood
Growing up in different cities but never feeling apart
And how I couldn't wait to see you each summer
So we could torment our parents with our antics
I could write about all those things and more
It's difficult to reduce or relationship into a mere poem
So for now let me say I love you
And I glad you are my little sister
You bring joy into my life

HAPPY BIRTHDAY!

EXISTENCE

I am a spiritual being
Living a human existence
I am mind, body, and spirit
I create beauty for my mind
Music, paintings, and song
I exercise for my body
To keep it strong and in tune
I seek spiritual enlightenment
For my soul
I allow my creator to use me
For His purpose
I say yes to his way
And yes to his will
And my existence stays in balance

MY DAILY PRAYER

Heavenly Father I thank you for this day
And your blessings that fill my life
I thank you for Christ Jesus
And His redemptive work on the cross
Paying the ultimate price for my sinful ways
I thank you for the Holy Spirit
Who guides me through my earthly journey
I am truly blessed to serve a God
Who takes care of my every need
Who feed me with truth and love
I pray you will continue to light my path
And I will always say
Yes to your way and yes to your will
I pray you continue to work
In and through my life
To use me for your glory
I pray you will give me
Mercy, strength, and guidance for my battles
And grace in my times of need
I pray for patience
So I will calmly wait upon you
And stillness so I will hear your voice
And let you be God all by yourself
In the name of Jesus Christ I pray
Amen

HEART OF GOLD

A WORD FROM THE AUTHOR

In 2009 memoirs or diaries as I call them, seemed to be flying off the book shelves; or maybe they were just filing them.

We all have stories to tell. Why should you read mine? Honestly, I don't know. Curiosity perhaps, intrigued by the prospect of a tall tale sure to dazzle you from a mysterious colorful person.
My life is not that interesting and I don't have that much to say. I'm what you call an average Joe. Besides, I'm not sure writer would be my handle, but very much a poet.

Poetry is my passion. Poetry is what helps keep me grounded and comforts me. It's my electric electric blanket on a cold winter night. So guess what, this ain't no memoir.

What you are reading now is one of a few satires I decided to throw in the book to dazzle you, yeah right! This is just a little something to loosen you up and give you a good laugh before you enjoy some romantic, heart felt, passionate, just may need a Kleenex poetry. That is of course if you read the back of the book first. Bad planning on my part, sorry.

Also, for the sake of posterity, for my daughter and grandkids. Maybe they will all look back one day and say he was a strange bird, but that's why we loved him.

I got the idea to add satires or letters in 2009 and I'm just getting around to it in 2021. I'm a late blooming baby boomer.

I was starting to realize in 2009 my life had been reduced to a bunch of timeless and golden cliques. Classics like, what doesn't kill you will make you stronger, It's not as long as it has been, this to shall pass, and I can show you better than I can tell you. You get the idea, the list is endless, and it seems now I'm showing my age.

It brought to mind an email I received from my sister over a decade prior. She was lamenting how strange her life has been.
Thus far it had seemed like a soap opera to her. I must admit her life did seem like a soap opera up to that point, and I could relate to that. Mine was headed in a dubious direction as well.

Talk about colorful people, Sis write a memoir I promise I'll read it. Being a good brother naturally I wanted to cheer her up, and make her laugh, so I came up with a crazy story of my own life. I entitled it The Obtuse Triangle. I tend to save most of what I write because I'm just crazy that way. I never know when or if it may come in handy. Good thing also, if I didn't you wouldn't have a chance to read it.

One last thing before we roll, my dear sister has become a successful, well balanced business woman all on her own as of 2021. Kudos to you Sis!

THE OBTUSE TRIANGLE

So, you're looking for a soap opera, huh.

While I was walking to the employee parking lot tonight I was thinking about my life. Not my entire life mind you, just a small part of it.

I have been blessed and I know that. However, when it comes to my love life, relationships and such, well, that's where the soap opera comes into play. I think it all started from birth, just kidding. I did say not my entire life, pay attention.

Let's start with my first marriage to the one and only Boo-boo the Fool, Ms. L. The snake in the wood pile that would sell her soul to the devil for a buck. If she had been a Viking she would have loved the pillage and plunder stuff. Spoiled rotten to the point she lied and stole from her own parents. In fact she once paid me to lie to them for her. I took the money, lied, and told her mother who wasn't shocked at all.
Go figure.

That marriage wasn't meant to last long and it didn't. I guess it was a bargain considering I have a wonderful daughter from the union and three fantastic grand children.

Then there was the divine Ms. M. Sweet as she could be. So sweet in fact she would not let me get divorced in peace. Kept pushing and pushing until I was in a corner. One day, I bit back like a rabid dog and ran away to suffer a horrible death. I've heard if you want a friend get a dog. Just not a rabid one of course.

How about the lovely Ms. A. The freak of the week that convinced me I was the real stud on the block. Oh daddy you're so big and last so long, how do you do it?

A woman that gave me everything I could ever want except a sentence that made sense. A woman that flies so high she encounters bird strikes that bring her crashing down to earth.
But not for long, then she is off again. Way to many take-offs and not enough landings. She use to be a stewardess, pun intended.

Ahhh yes, my darling Ms. C, vintage 1991. Oh what a year that was for a tequila guzzling myopic man like me. Doomed from the start, thousands of miles between us but love will keep us alive.

Scene 1 - Act 5, he finds the love in his heart is more than his soul could bear. He thinks he is faster than a speeding bullet, more powerful than a locomotive, able to leap large states with a single bound. Buddy, get a grip will you! And here we are after years of separation looking at miles once again. Hey it's nice to have an old friend that still loves me what can I say.

Now let's see, the wonderful Ms. G. You know that screwed up blonde from some weird island far far away. Nobody is getting off this island alive. And if you do you'll be crazy for sure. Don't you all know the world revolves around me? You have to be stupid not to know that. I am so misunderstood. I am a good person all my friends tell me I am why can't you see it? Oh what the heck, my next stop is the twilight zone.

Well, looking at my watch I see there is time for yet another "E" ticket ride. I know, let's go crash the convent I must have said to myself. Let's go pick up a nun that's sure to be wild.

Thus my second marriage to another Ms. L follows ten years later. Wait a minute, another "L" am I crazy. Dare I try this again. Didn't I learn the first time, I guess not. I had better be carful she just may knock the "L" out of me.

I haven't been with a man in so long because I am scared to try again. Just give me some time and lots of it pal. In the meantime I'll cook for you everyday so you'll get fat and nobody will want your fat ass but me. We will hold hands on occasion, and after one kiss if you finally get one, we'll be boyfriend and girlfriend. My goodness is this the way it's done in the new millennium. Run Karl, run for the hills as fast as you can this is your first clue buddy. Then Karl I'll dump you after a while because you know I'm not going to grow. I know you'll get bored with me because I like my life in a small box. I couldn't get so lucky ten years later…oh brother!

You know, I've heard of folks life going full circle, but mine seems like an obtuse triangle…and so it goes.

PARENTS

It's a beautiful July afternoon and I'm sitting poolside with a good book in my hands. I pause for a moment to think about my parents, my mother in particular.
I'm thinking what a lucky man I am to have had two wonderful parents who always loved me. Two parents who gave me a good life, a life with joy and happiness. A rebirth if you will, starting over, breathing room and a sense of security.

I guess I should back up a bit and mention my parents are hanging out with God in heaven as I write this. You would never know it as much as I talk with them. Their spirit lives in and around me always.

Don't get me wrong I'm not sitting around feeling depressed because they passed on. I've gotten comfortable with it, finally.

I'm thinking of their legacy. Their footprint on my heart and my life, how much they meant to me. I'm thinking of all the love they quietly and thoughtfully gave me without question or doubt. Love, what a legacy!

I have experienced so much growth and understanding since they pass away and worked through the grief. It was only then I was able to set into motion all of the life lessons they taught me along the way.

HOSTAGE

Listening to the voice of reason on a long distance line. A very dear friend, an ex-lover, a woman of strength and wisdom. She's the one I truly need and want in my life. Where did we go wrong? Oh yeah the distance, coast to coast, among other things out of our control.

So I'm listening and thinking of the distance in a local woman. Distance in heart and mind. A local woman who would free me to stay in my own head, as she stays lost and selfish in hers. However, this is not the code I live by.

The voice of reason that I need so much speaks loudly, and makes so much more sense that anything I have ever heard. More than anything going through my mind.

Should I reach out for that one dimensional, one layer lady. Use her to spring board deep into the reality that makes me write dark and introspective poems of real life. I pine for her while I wait in vain, waiting for the impossible. Waiting for my one layer twisted muse of sort to grow into life with me. A rather smart idea I must say after all these years of being familiar.

I wait for her to grow into a beautiful multi faceted woman. Grow into someone of great depth. Move into emotional waters beyond herself. Learn to be honest, learn to trust in herself, to believe I am exactly what she needs in her life. I am the better alternative, and no one understands her more than I do. Our sorted history speaks volumes.

Sadly, I am beginning to realize this compromise is worth everything, and nothing in the same breathe. Ay my age I realize this may be my calling to write dark introspective poetry. Poems with a taste of sunshine and hope weaved within the darkness.

My one layer lady leaves me wanting more of what she can not give me. And this muse of sort propels me into the darkness that bring my writing alive; though my soul truly lives in the light. Her soul seems empty and cold as her heart. Vanity has made her blind.
Can I really sell myself out? Can I sell my soul for a pound of flesh just to get inspired? Or, do I do the right thing and stay in the light?
Everything and nothing in the same breathe.

This may be my last stand to get it all done. To explore my passions, to live out my dreams and desires. I have more day's behind me than in front of me. Ironically, at her age it just may be her last stand as well.

From the outside looking in I see her squandering her life away in a lose-lose relationship with a man she doesn't like anymore but can't let go. A relationship she hangs onto for dear life in pain and agony as if she feels this is all she is worth and deserves.

After every break-up there always seems to be the false hope of something left behind. Something missing, something left to save.

Perhaps we are both being held hostage by our own devices.

MS. C Tail end of a letter sent explaining my cancer story.

I have never met anyone with your wit and charm, grace and beauty, heart, soul, and sincerity since you.

I have never bonded with anyone in quite the same way we bonded. Looking back at the magical moments in the Bahamas we grew together and bonded so fast. We shared so much together in such a short period of time. Though we never made love we shared love from our hearts, no flesh required, just our hearts. How sweet it was! Thinking about it now is just like old times but with new meaning. I still get goose bumps.

I thank the universe and my lucky stars for our meeting. I feel blessed for all the wonderful years that followed. Nothing happens by chance, but by design. Those wonderful years have made us the friends we still are today.

When we met you set the bar high just by being you. It's a beautiful thing and I have alway loved you for it. I compared other woman to you and none ever matched up. Just being wonderful loving you brought so much joy into my life, and it continues to this day. You still give love in every facet of it's meaning. What a wonderful woman you are.

I look forward to a time when I can hold you in my arms again, look into your gorgeous brown eyes, and tell you how much I still cherish and adore you. I will never stop loving you my darling.

I can't thank you enough for reaching out to me this year. I'm going over a bump in the road and knowing you are there for me fills my heart with hope. Your phone calls and cards, wow, I can hardly find the words to express how much they mean to me.

I know you care about me and I feel blessed for it. This will help me get through my cancer journey.

MS. C Admiration and Thank You.

When I met you on the evening of 9/13/91 I was exhausted from a long and brutal trip to the Bahamas. I remember sitting in the lobby of the concert venue saying to myself, go to your room, get some rest and figure it out tomorrow.

Then David walked towards me with three lovely ladies and my eyes fixed on you. He introduced you all and I couldn't stop looking at you. We spoke briefly and I was at a loss for words. But I knew I just had to see you again when I was rested.

You told me you and your friends would be at the beach front in the morning so come on down. I though about you all night and couldn't wait to see you on the beach the following day.

I could sense in our brief encounter in the lobby you were an extraordinary woman and I had to get to know you. When I saw you the next day basking in the morning sun on your lounge chair I was excited. Then the magic began.

I started to fall in love with you that day. There was a moment when you really trusted this strange beige man you just met and that meant the world to me.

We were walking along the the beach and I asked you if you wanted to get in the water. You said no thanks, and mentioned that you couldn't swim. The next thing we knew you were floating on the surface on the water in my arms. Thus, began my love for you.

I have relived that moment countless times since that day. Trust is earned and not always given. But you trusted me as I held your body above the water line so you wouldn't sink. You relaxed in my arms and I was in heaven.

You looked magnificent, just gorgeous. Beautiful golden hair, and the silver bangles on your arm were shimmering in the water as your skin was beginning to bronze in the island sun. It was magic.
I started falling in love with you that day and my love has grown ever since. I have never stopped loving you and never will. I am so blessed to have found my soul mate.

I know you love me there is no doubt about it. You have been my friend, rock, lover, and inspiration for nearly thirty years. And last week you proved it once again by offering to care for me in my time of need. To give me love and support and help me recover from the cancer that has taken residence in my body. I can't thank you enough. I am a blessed man to have a friend like you.

I'm going to try a less radical treatment plan for now and pray it works. A stem cell transplant sounds crazy to me with no guarantee it will work. Knowing you have my back and I can take you up on your offer should I change my mind make my decision easier.

Thank you my love :)

LAVENDER MIDST

MIDNIGHT SKY

CHOPPY SEA

SPRING FORTH

HALLOWEEN TREAT

SOMEWHERE IN THE DESERT

SAGUARO GARDEN

SEASCAPE

MOTHERS TEACHING MOMENT